CYRIL AND THE DINNER PARTY

by Michael Palin

ILLUSTRATED BY CAROLINE HOLDEN

PUFFIN BOOKS

Cyril was quite an ordinary boy, except that he had the power to turn people into other things just by looking at them.

He had first discovered this magic power at the age of three when he had turned an aunt, whom he didn't like much, into an ornamental clock.

Only for a second or two, but it was enough. One minute she was telling him to keep his elbows off the table while eating, the next she was up on the mantelpiece alongside the other clock. Uncle Frank noticed at once . . .

'Beatrice,' he said to Cyril's mother, 'do my eyes deceive
me or are there two clocks on your mantelpiece?'

'Don't be so silly Frank,' she scolded, 'as if anyone would
want *two* clocks on the same mantelpiece.' Sure enough,
when he looked again there was only one, and Auntie Vi was
back at the table.

'Tick-tock!' she said cheerfully.
Uncle Frank looked up. 'What did you say dear?'
'Tick-tock, tick-tock, ping!' replied Auntie Vi.

All the grown-ups looked at each other, then went on eating.

'Are you going to vote Liberal again this year?' said Uncle Arnold conversationally.

'Cuckoo' said Auntie Vi.

'Are you all right, dear?' said Auntie Emily, who was the nice one.

'Ding-dong, ding-dong, ding-dong. Bong! Bong!'

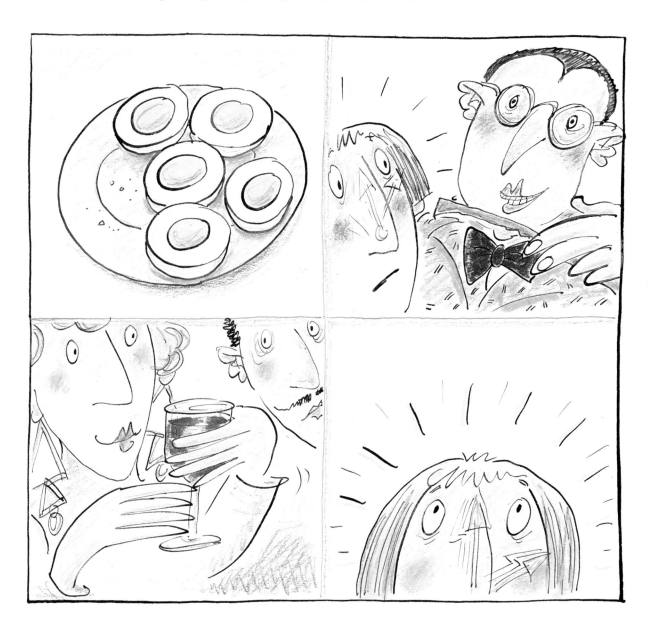

Cyril was quite bored by now, so he decided to turn his grandfather, who never said much anyway, into a seal, just as a diversion.

There was a flurry of activity at grandfather's end of the table, and they all turned away from looking at Auntie Vi.

'I say!' exclaimed Uncle Frank, 'there isn't a seal in the house is there?'

'Don't be so silly' said Cyril's mother sharply . . .

'Dong!' continued Auntie Vi.

'. . . seals don't run about in people's houses.'

'I saw one go behind the television' said Uncle Frank.

'Most unlikely,' said Cyril's mother.

'Oink-oink!' said grandfather very loudly.

'Dong!' said Auntie Vi.

'This is most peculiar,' said Uncle Frank.

At which point Cyril turned him into a huge parrot; just for
a second, but long enough for Mr Margerison, the family
solicitor, to gulp horribly on a mouthful of fish which he spat
out between clenched teeth.

'Mr Margerison,' said Cyril's mother in alarm, 'whatever's the matter?'

'I swear I saw a parrot.'

'On the television?' said Auntie Emily with interest.

'Dong!' said Auntie Vi.

'Oink!' answered grandfather.

'Who's a pretty boy then?' said Uncle Frank twice.

'I think he's probably gone mad,' said Cyril's mother, 'first seeing a seal, and then saying things like that.'

Cyril didn't like his mother saying that about Uncle Frank so he turned her into a terrible smell.

'Oink!' went grandfather.

'Dong!' went Auntie Vi.

'Who's a pretty boy then?' said Uncle Frank.

'Pooh!' said Auntie Emily, 'what's that terrible smell?'

'Probably something's died under the floorboard,' said Mr Margerison who, being a solicitor, was quite tactful.

'I think the Conservatives are still the only practical alternative,' said Uncle Arnold, his last words, as it turned out, before he turned into Long John Silver.

'Tick-tock, tick-tock,' said Auntie Vi.
'Oink!' shouted grandfather.
'Who's a pretty boy then?' shouted Uncle Frank.
'Dong!' said Auntie Vi.
'Ahoy!' said Uncle Arnold.

The terrible smell got worse.
And no-one noticed Mr Margerison turn into a barn owl
and flap up onto one of the pictures.

'To-Whit, To-Whoo' said the family solicitor.
'Is that a legal term?' said Auntie Emily to Mr Margerison helpfully.

23

'There'll be keelhaulings if we don't make Hispaniola by nightfall!' shouted Uncle Arnold.

'Who's a pretty boy then?' said Uncle Frank.

'Oink' said grandfather.

Cyril turned his father into a hot tap.

'Is it the smell you're worried about?' asked Auntie Emily, who was getting confused.

'Drip-Drip-Drip' went Cyril's father.

'Erk Erk!' went Mrs Margerison.

Cyril was very pleased with what he had done with Mrs
Margerison. She was always rather a pest . . . wanting to
kiss him all the time, and he enjoyed seeing her as an ostrich.

'Erk!' she said again.

'Dong!' said Auntie Vi.

'Drip-Drip-Drip' went Cyril's father.

'Belay the mainbrace, or you'll swing!' shouted Uncle Arnold.

'Oink!' said grandfather.

'Who's a pretty boy then,' said Uncle Frank.

'To-Whit, To-Whoo!' said Mr Margerison.

Cyril looked at Auntie Emily and shrugged:
'Grown-ups!' he said.
And he turned her into a little girl again.